CHRONICLE OF AN OBSESSION:

LOVE, DEATH, AND THE PROSTATE

poems by

David C. Meyer

Finishing Line Press
Georgetown, Kentucky

CHRONICLE OF AN OBSESSION:

LOVE, DEATH, AND THE PROSTATE

Copyright © 2025 by David C. Meyer
ISBN 979-8-89990-100-3 First Edition
All rights reserved under International and Pan-American Copyright Conventions. No part of this book may be reproduced in any manner whatsoever without written permission from the publisher, except in the case of brief quotations embodied in critical articles and reviews.

ACKNOWLEDGMENTS

"Anti-cancer Janus Machine" was published in the online journal *First Literary Review—East*. It also appeared as a reprint in the print journal *Cape Rock*.
"Apologia pro Poemate Meo" received a commendation by the O'Donaghue International Prize, Cork, Ireland.
"November, French Creek" accepted for future publication in *Gray's Sporting Journal*.
This manuscript, *Chronicle of an Obsession*, was a finalist for the *Fjords Review* chapbook contest, 2023.

Publisher: Leah Huete de Maines
Editor: Christen Kincaid
Cover Art: R.K. Courtney
Author Photo: David C. Meyer
Cover Design: Elizabeth Maines McCleavy

Order online: www.finishinglinepress.com
also available on amazon.com

Author inquiries and mail orders:
Finishing Line Press
PO Box 1626
Georgetown, Kentucky 40324
USA

Contents

Key Facts About the Prostate Gland that May Be Useful in Reading These Poems 1
Appologia pro Poemate Meo 3
The Ritual of Sentencing 4
Love and the Carnal Aptitudes 5
Robot Guerilla 6
Anti-cancer Janus Machine 7
Longing for the Resurrection 8
Post-op Itch 9
Seasons 10
Two-faced Test Results 11
New Studies Cast Doubt 12
Time and the Scalpel's Edge 13
Janus, or The Fantasy of Other Women Lost 15
Loving Flesh 17
Still Desiring You 18
Death in Little Things 19
November, French Creek 20
Thanks 21
Begging the Absolution Question 22
Growing Old Together 23
If Not 24
Still Waiting 25
A Glance 26
Love in Early November 27
Almost Midnight 28
Flaming Out 29
Winter Come … 30
And Yet, and Yet, the snake's seduction isn't all … 31
Except 32

Author Biography 33

for Wendy Foster, M.D.
whose care felt that first suspicious nodule

and, as always,
for my longsuffering
Pat

KEY FACTS ABOUT THE PROSTATE GLAND
THAT MAY BE USEFUL IN READING THESE POEMS

Because most male readers below a certain age and many women regardless of age cannot be expected to know much about the anatomy and physiology of the prostate gland, here is a very brief summary which may help those readers:

The prostate gland, often described as slightly larger than and resembling a walnut, is located in men's lower body cavity above the peritoneum. It wraps around the urethra between the bladder and the penis. About two thirds of the gland's tissue consists of tiny wormlike ducts that produce the prostatic fluid; the remaining third is muscles that help control both urine flow and ejaculation. The nerves managing blood circulation and constriction in the penis, and hence erection, are wrapped around the outer sheath of the prostate. These nerves are vulnerable to irreparable injury during either surgical removal or radiation treatment of the prostate, hence the danger of impotence and incontinence after these interventions for prostate cancer. Modern nerve-sparing surgical techniques have radically reduced, but not totally eliminated, the risk of damage to these nerves. One reason for this risk of damage is that some tumors grow too close to the surface of the prostate itself (and hence these nerves) for the nerves to be spared.

Many prostate surgeries are now done robotically. There is no firm evidence of reduced nerve damage in robotic surgery, though there are numerous other advantages to this technology.

Prostate cancer effects one man in six and is the second most common cause of cancer death among men. However, it is also among the most treatable of all cancers in men. Nearly 50% of men who reach the age of 80 will be diagnosed with prostate cancer. Erectile dysfunction, though dramatically less common than in the past, still effects some men treated for prostate cancer, though it is often helped or completely alleviated by a variety of ED therapies. Almost all post-surgical recovery of erectile function occurs within two years following surgery. After that interval, further recovery is possible, but improbable.

* * *

The Dr. Foster to whom I refer in "Familiar" is **not** Wendy Foster, to whom this chapbook is dedicated. For about 25 years Wendy was my internist, whereas the Dr. Foster of the poem was my pediatrician as a child. They are not related.

CHRONICLE OF AN OBSESSION:
LOVE, DEATH, AND THE PROSTATE

APOLOGIA PRO POEMATE MEO

My words grunt obscenities. So?
Cancer does that to the mind.
Wrestling death, I win the fall,
but lose the splendor in my groin

because I win. The shared delight
that was my lover joined with me
shrivels into memory.
Cancer does that to the flesh.

These poems mean their curses, cumless
sweats, and piss dribbled on toes,
their sharpened stick rammed in your bum's
eye. Offended? Clench your ass,

your mind. Otherwise, read on:
cancer does this to the heart:

THE RITUAL OF SENTENCING

After the 'digital' exam, he says,
"The cancer's nestled on a critical nerve
at the gland's edge. I'll do what I can to spare it,
but whether I can or not, I can't predict.
Enough to preserve erectile function?" He shrugs.
'Erectile function.' Analytic term
for an un-analytic yearning for
the lover's tool to stand up for pleasure.

By ancient tradition judges placed a black
silk square on their wig before a sentence of Death.
But this is only Death to the little death,
so maybe saving an actual life has made
the hand with the black cloth withdraw, not
unlike the tissue it may soon condemn.

LOVE AND THE CARNAL APTITUDES

These poems want to bind up grief for a lost
prostate sent to a lone pathologist
who stalks death disguised in tissue and blood.
Rhymes yawp; wooden rhythms bludgeon
virgin pages. I rage against erection's
ardor severed with the gland's resection,
rage against my shredded nerves, and the parting
of our lovers' flesh from our loving hearts.

These wanton lines send up, not nostalgia
for the carnal aptitudes the surgeon
cut, but rather a fey and artless hope
your tender touch can mend my frayed rope,
tying my scarred flesh with yours, just
as our bodies bound our souls in ages past.

ROBOT GUERILLA

Tiny half-tracked APCs
grinding through my guts force
a light where darkness lurked before,
searching out the death in me,

their mission to destroy
my killer cells—like Vietnam,
its famished black pajamas doomed
to stalk our green-clad, well-fed boys

who, in turn, stalked *them* to make
them light as ghosts. Or be made light.
Within my groin the robot fights
for me. Cancer cannot break

those creaking treads, nor dull those blades.
It may, of course, creep off and wait.

ANTI-CANCER JANUS MACHINE

The robot's built to cut it out, and with
that cut to part me for a while from death.

But nothing comes so singly beneficial:
blades the clever-crawling engine slipped

between my guts and groin parted nerves
as well, paring love to just a word

without a deed, its intimate intent
intact, its mechanism disconnected.

LONGING FOR THE RESURRECTION

So now we wait, week after week,
month after month, for piss to stop
its drip, drip, drip, the prick to find
its legs, stand up, and be a man.

Forgive this fallen flesh, my love.
The prostate's such a lovely thing
until it's not. Its plot against
my life condemned, it wreaks revenge

on you as well: my damaged vessel's
failure to be filled compelling
your undamaged vessel to
be slighted, fondled by a stand-in.

When, oh when will this damned droop
find its courage and stand up?

POST-OP ITCH

'Lead in your pencil,' the poet's goal,
instrument for scrawling passion
on my Patti's parchment flesh
in characters of love and hope.

But if the scalpel nicked that fun,
the craving-scratcher of delight
betrayed, the lover's itch defiled,
the purple-poem deed undone?

Then my pencil scribbles nil,
its only hope a fucking pill.

SEASONS

Where once my penis painted stars
in the velvet dark beneath your womb,
urgent teens in the back of a car
on a rainy April afternoon—

how long since we needed to lie
in that back seat? Now robot blades
have carved that springtime from our lives
and left instead this dull ache,

these unexpected drips of urine
in my shorts, this long goodbye
to you squeezing my fattened worm
as it burrowed its way between your thighs.

Even last year.... So, we've come to this:
a dry, disembodied November kiss.

TWO-FACED TEST RESULTS

My cancer 'undetectable,' we dance
as if on a floor strewn with orange blossoms
at a wedding where we trample out
desire's perfume. But, finding the surgeon's
death-delaying dance has trampled nerves
as well, and yearning for the brothy scent
of passion with its *little* death, I
almost regret surviving in damaged flesh.

NEW STUDIES CAST DOUBT

on whether the cancerous prostate—thicket
of ducts tangling life with death,

affliction's tendrils spreading slowly
as tree-roots in dense clay—truly

requires the knife. But mine, excised
before such happy findings, ends

in the waste, leaving us longing for wood.

      *   *   *

But passion, kept intact, frightened,
yet still able to act, might've

roused yearnings in you for a fate
hard as bloody life, ejaculate

burning through our wait for death.
Now our fucking must depend

on dampened nerves for catching fire.

TIME AND THE SCALPEL'S EDGE

    1

I wait, still, for the soft failed stem
to thrive, possessed by its purpled fruit, its promise
of gnarled veins vining round a stem
to reconstruct a way for us to climb,
albeit by appointment with a sky-blue
pharmaceutical. And then, well ...

Nothing—No! Sensation. Your moist tongue

around my sweet plum in the afternoon,
your lips pressing it for juices unlike
either a noble vintage or a perry ...

    2

Yet, with age, you too incline toward earth:
Rosy petals' browned with thirst, their folds
dried and crisp at the edges, no longer able
to brew their richly scented, healing tea ...

Pushing the glans home, if it could
push home, in this desiccated flower
would plant a thorn in flesh I once made weep
with pleasure. Thus, time and the scalpel's edge

have grafted into us this latest fruit,
frosted, withered, about to fall. Even
so, come. Sit. Take ease and drink.

3

Give us a kiss. Oh! It tastes of today,
of juices pushed through gnarled vines, about
to yield their final, old-growth harvest, dry,
full-bodied, long on the palate, with hints of loam.

JANUS, or Imagination's Fancywomen Lost

    1   baby face

O nipple actuated mound,
O plump and dimpled ass rounded

on the warm, dank well
where musky female perfumes dwell

with sticky, stinky invitation
to the fever-bred sensation

of, not love, but craving slaked
in soggy flesh. O perfect mate,

no matter who. O perfect meat
in which my dagger stabs its heat,

thrusting for the Little Death
in any sheath. But then the Big Death

comes, fucking baby's dreams.

2   grown-up face

Now I dare ask only *you* to breathe

life into the shriveled carcass laid
between my legs, worm after a rain

drying on the sidewalk in the sun.
Could I expect a sex-mirage to run

her tongue along its withered skin, lip
its head, strain miraculous muscles in

a vain attempt to make the old guy young,
as if this thing might still fill-up her fun?

Only you, my constant love, can share
such wounded need, can twist our curse and care

in a single silken cord that binds up loss
and softly leads me from my bloody lust.

LOVING FLESH

Tongues and fingers search, eyes
probe, breath a shared stagger,
legs coiling round each other
in the antic Dance of the Little

Death—But now, passion in rags,
my former, firmer flesh will not
let me be! And yet, even
with this vagrant raging, I

am not my penis only, not
its semen spill undone, nor
its new *de minimis* tumescence.
No. In this disheveled self

of mine, love's touch still survives
to wake a whispered bliss in you.

STILL DESIRING YOU

If, like a butcher, the surgeon hacked
all—not the prostate only, no,
but penis, testicles, urethra,
even the secret winding channels

of the mind wherein our feral
cravings touch affection, truly
all in other words—then
perhaps the eunuch's sort of peace:

flesh reduced to dumplings stewed
too long in blessed memory.

But how could I confuse this post-
operative lover's ache with just

the absence of desiring you?
Even with the hard core
of cancer in my coil excised
and penetration pared to thrusts

of grudging recollection, your
brothy presence rises to
my nostrils, building up my heart
with marrow's strength that lives in bone.

DEATH IN LITTLE THINGS
for Grayson

For the first time I catch
a whiff of stale urine
rising from my pants.
Can the boy beside me
smell its taint as well?

Its acrid tang of aging
lifts like steam from snow-soaked
wool corrupting a winter
subway car. Like,
except for the mortification.

NOVEMBER, FRENCH CREEK

I settle a fly in the lane and hope
for the rise, the flash, the dazzle of speckles
chased on a bronze flank. But

when I step deeper into the pool,
my waders leak an ice stiletto
into the groin where I was cut,

pricking the memory of love,
of the time before the knife: a balance
point between the warmth of a whole
past and the withering cold to come.

THANKS

This new, flaccid sort of climax reaches
us with slow care, as if you peeled
an over-ripened plum that, in a gentle
wind, let go its burdened branch and sent
itself with countless others to purple the earth.
You take it up, measuring its worth:
If left, might bees hover to sip its juices?
Can sweet joy be had from flesh so ... loose?

You know it can't, and yet, and yet ...
You find there *is* another kind of pleasure,
one that thrums the nerves without the mess,
without the hardened stem, the sting's excess.
You find devotion's labor leads to this
release, earning us both a honeyed bliss.

BEGGING THE ABSOLUTION QUESTION

Forgive me, Patti, for I have sinned
against your maiden blush, your winning
smile, the flesh-made pleasure pinned

between us—vulva finger-spread,
and groans, and stumbled love bled
of its sticky joy on a rumpled bed—

O! forgive my crumpled prick!
And all that heart of us tricked out
in florid poems forced to bid

erection fond farewell, alas.
Forgive my fallen, damaged man,
my words of shattered mirror glass

tearing our once private blessings
into bloody, public shreds
that leave you red with my obsession.

GROWING OLD TOGETHER

All that peach fuzz in the tender brain
where green affection dreams a ripe future;
all that ready flesh crushed, that juice
dripping down the chin, that sweetness … Sure.

'Growing old together,' formula
of innocents and teary parents needing
the kids to have a better time of it
than they have. Soon enough the blood in the brain

clots, the thyroid sprouts its nodes, prostate
its malignant seed, the disused womb
its cist. So this is how it ends: cells
forgetting how to live, autumn's flesh

dug under in the garden where the drowsy
bee has come to sting apples, the cabbage
worm to gnaw its grave in gnarled leaves.
And we've come here as well, to savor all.

IF NOT

the creepers of this canker-cancer,
other deaths will weave
their tendrils in between
the nerves and muscles of our dance,

choking off the love that starts
the air with song, the thrum
that strikes the heart's drum,
the calves flexed, the arches taut

with present joy on a naked stage.
Thus, a sure and certain end will short
the passion that our touch exhorts
in flesh, will shrivel it with age,

will deaden nerves with grit, grinding
love's hard pleasures into sand.

STILL WAITING

Years add up. After a long
sit, knees won't kick,
the back unbend, the balance hold.
Toes crack like sticks.

Memories of easy motion
die in gritty dreams.
Only the prick, snug in its wrinkles,
stays, unstiff and lean.

LOVE IN EARLY NOVEMBER

I

My penis matters. And your vagina.
Your labia, my testicles.
Our lips and nipples, eyes and tongues.
They all matter, the named and unnamed

parts St. Paul condemned as *sarx,*
flesh, the carnal thread of love's
addiction stitching us forever
in our lone selves. They matter.

But still, side-by-side night
after night, the moist and hard of youth
retired by time, disease, the knife
No. We're more than damaged parts.

II

Two elms (cleaved so long together
neither can be fed or parched
without the other) shed blizzards
of yellow leaves mimicking death

until, drawing the night's silence
into their weary groans, their long
arms scratching the sky with a million
fingers, they beckon snow to come.

A GLANCE

at your descending tits, your thinning pubes,
your buns drooping down the decades, and
I lift. My over-buckle gut, my stoop,
my fallen face, heart on its leaky slosh
toward peace, all but the drooping dick

lift, for love's a flesh beyond flesh failed,
beyond the settling into earth, the penis
drooped, vagina parched. With just this tender
glance to urge us up the stairs, we start
our wishful climb panting toward paradise.

ALMOST MIDNIGHT

Marking my page, I pull
the lamp's chain and turn
to you. Early summer
sidles through the screen,
wooing my naked, tired
old man's withered flesh,

erecting your old woman's
nipples, tempting my fingers,
my tongue. But it's been years
since the knife excising cancer
from my groin, also
nicked erection's nerves,

years of losing hope
in the blood stirred by breath
and lips and fingertips.
Only a vague thickness
recalls such flesh, such taut,
purpled skin, the tender

snake let loose. But even
on this summer's eve
the starved beast persists,
secreted in its hole,
gnawing at what's left
of me, of you, of us.

FLAMING OUT

The years since the robot cut my cancer out
can't heal us. My pleasure stem wilted on
your tongue exhausts your pursed lips; my finger
pressing your dried pleasure bud prompts
just pain. Flesh-love failed, need nods off.
Thus, carnal life flickers and goes out.

Two ancients, side-by-side, heads on pillows
remembering their bed as a pyre of love,
as chaos smelting joy from mortal metal,
one arched above the other, their fire sparking
before the aching back and the dampened
nerves extinguished all that. Passion snuffed,

we scatter ash on its casket, pray a final
wild prayer of loving, and step away.

WINTER COME …

skin to skin undone
touch gone cold   fall's final reds
buried in new snow

AND YET, AND YET, THE SNAKE'S SEDUCTION ISN'T ALL …

or even half. There is, as well,
the streetlight's cone, the winter night,
cold so cold it hardens aging
snow to marble slabs while new

flat flakes begin their flutter
down through the ice-bright air, a veil
drawn across the paling lamp
as dawn begins to soften dark.

I turn to you snuggled beside me
and give thanks for love's long pleasures,
the to-ing and fro-ing of summers and winters,
the mumbling back and forth of decades,

the flesh and failed flesh of us
ancients tucked beneath our friendly
down and peeking out as shards
of starlight settle through the night.

But then, in the dark at the top of the stairs,
warmed by the comforter's down, we
reach out, fingers slowly stirring
our moist, delicate parts, which

from these almost forgotten strokes
spiral into shudders we
had thought only memory
could summon out of our loving past.

EXCEPT

to be … summoned for a moment
on a winter's night is not
to be summoned for forever. Love's billion
burning cells whiten to ash,

their final glow trampled by that
forever which crushes all, the flesh,
the billion-celled love, and even time
itself compacted into diamonds.

David Meyer has always been a late bloomer, starting with his birth 45 days late! His parents, a theatre director and a house painter, divorced 11 months later! Now 81, he's recently completed four poetry ms.: three chapbooks, plus the book-length narrative *The Lotus War: Never In-country*. He is currently working on a book of outdoor poems tentatively titled *The Man In Love With Silence*, and a full-length play called *The Pleasure Bargain* set in a WW II concentration camp brothel.

Though an Iowa native, Meyer has lived most of his life in Chicago. In the '60s he entered seminary to evade the Vietnam War, thereby diverting himself from his true vocation as a poet and playwright. After unsatisfactory stints as a university English Instructor and a Unitarian Minister, he pursued book publishing, eventually founding a liberal theological publishing house (yes, there is such a thing). He is grateful that, when the publishing house went under because of insufficient capitalization, inattention to cash flow, and a few misguided publishing decisions, his wife Pat had a good job teaching English, so Dave lost neither her nor their house (both uncertain for a time). Since retiring from his publishing career, Dave has focused on poetry and playwriting, progressive politics, international travel, peace through friendship, fly-fishing, and Pat. Always Pat.

Education: B.A. (Theatre), M.A. (writing/17th Century drama and poetry), University of Northern Iowa; M.Div., Garrett Theological Seminary [Northwestern University]; M.A. Theological Studies, Meadville Theological School [University of Chicago]; M.F.A., Writing (poetry/fiction), Vermont College of Fine Arts.

Teachers/Mentors in poetry and writing: At U.N.I. the late James Hearst and the late Robley Wilson; at V.C.F.A. Robin Behn, Douglas Glover, Cynthia Huntington, and Walter Wetherell; plus, in the V.C.F.A. post-graduate seminars, Bruce Weigl and the late Michael Steinberg. Private tutorials in poetry manuscript development: Roger Weingarten and Leslie Ullman. Leslie's careful reading and attention to book structure were of great assistance in arriving at the final ms. of *The Lotus War*.

Teachers/Mentors in Playwriting: At Chicago Dramatists, June Pyskacek and the late Russ Tutterow; at Victory Gardens Theatre, Douglas Post and Claudia Allen. Private tutorials in playwriting/play development: Douglas Post, Claudia Allen, and John Clinton Eisner.

Meyer has published over 100 poems, a few essays, and one play. His chapbook *Chronicle of an Obsession: Love, Death, and the Prostate*, forthcoming from Finishing Line Press, was also a finalist in the *Fjords Review* chapbook competition. Another chapbook *Congregation of the Damned: a Chapbook of Evasion* (excerpts from The Lotus War) received a 'high commendation' in The Munster Literature Centre's (Cork, Ireland) "Fool for Poetry International Chapbook Award." His poem "Apologia pro Poemate Meo" received 'commendation' from The Munster Literature Centre's O'Donaghue International Prize; his poem "The Blessing Way" won the Ruth Cable Prize from ELF: the Eclectic Literary Forum. his poem "Between the Night and its Mirror" (published as "Night") won honorable mention from the *Rambunctious Review* annual contest.

In addition to publications, Meyer has had a play produced at the University of Northern Iowa, another given a table reading at Writers' Theatre Chicago, and a third given a staged reading at Circle Theatre Chicago.

In the '90s, Meyer was first a reader, then on the four-person editorial board for the late, lamented *River Oak Review*.

www.ingramcontent.com/pod-product-compliance
Lightning Source LLC
Chambersburg PA
CBHW020220090426
42734CB00008B/1143